my guide to space exploration

Rover

Cherry Lake Press

Published in the United States of America by Cherry Lake Publishing Group
Ann Arbor, Michigan
www.cherrylakepublishing.com

Reading Adviser: Beth Walker Gambro, MS, Ed., Reading Consultant, Yorkville, IL
Book Design: Jennifer Wahl
Illustrator: Joseph Hatch

Photo Credits: NASA/JPL-Caltech, 5; © Willams Harking/Shutterstock, 7; NASA/JPL-Caltech/MSSS, 9; NASA/JPL-Caltech, 11; © Juan Jose Tugores/Dreamstime.com, 13; NASA/JPL-Caltech/Cornell Univ./Arizona State Univ., 15; NASA/JPL-Caltech, 17; © Triff/Shutterstock, 19; NASA/JPL-Caltech, 21; NASA/JPL-Caltech/Univ. of Arizona, 23

Cherry Lake Press is an imprint of Cherry Lake Publishing Group

Library of Congress Cataloging-in-Publication Data has been filed and is available at catalog.loc.gov

Printed in the United States of America

table of contents

About the author: Samantha Bell was born and raised near Orlando, Florida. She grew up in a family of eight kids and all kinds of pets, including goats, chickens, cats, dogs, rabbits, horses, parakeets, hamsters, guinea pigs, a monkey, a raccoon, and a coatimundi. She now lives with her family in the foothills of the Blue Ridge Mountains, where she enjoys hiking, painting, and snuggling with their cats Pocket, Pebble, and Mr. Tree-Tree Triggers.

About the illustrator: Joseph Hatch is the art director for Tilbury House Publishers. He holds a degree in Graphic Design and Illustration from Madison College in Madison, Wisconsin. An illustrator, painter, and certified Michigan master naturalist, Joseph can usually be found at home organic gardening, beekeeping, growing edible mushrooms, planting native plants, and either building, fixing, or playing stringed instruments. He lives in Ann Arbor, Michigan, with his wife, their two children, a house cat, two dogs, nine chickens, and fifty thousand honeybees.

About Rovers

I'm a rover. I'm a small robot. I move. I help **scientists**. We study space.

Some rovers go to the Moon. Some go to **asteroids**. I go to Mars.

I gather rocks.
I do **experiments**.

I have many cameras. Some take pictures.

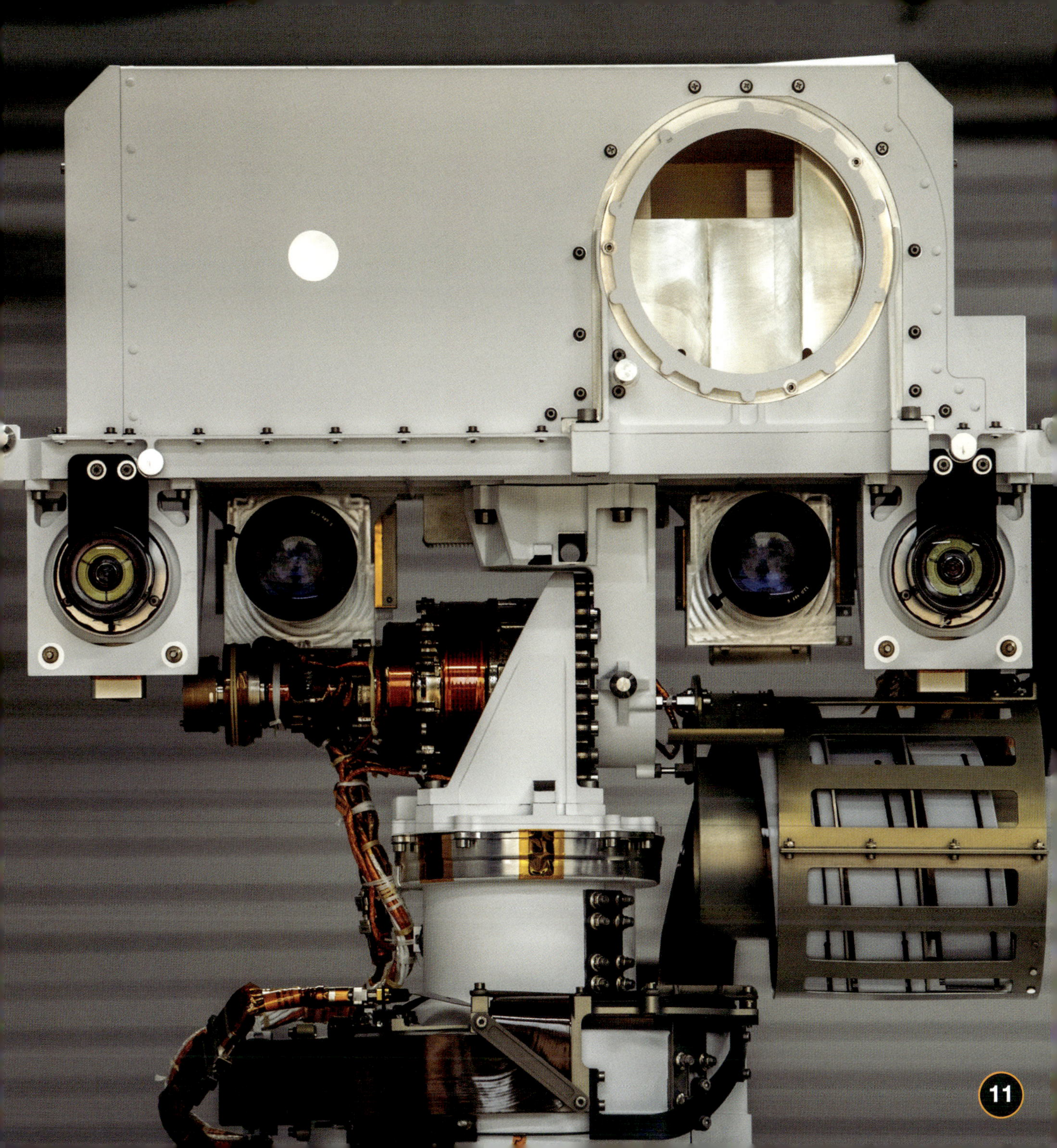

Some act like eyes. They help me **navigate**.

I have **solar panels**. I get energy. It is from the Sun.

NASA
JPL

I store the energy. I keep it in batteries. They power me.

J2
J1
2037MOXELX J1
10250482-1

I have six wheels. The wheels are big. They have thick **tread**. They work on rocky land.

My arms hold tools. I use the tools. I collect **data**. I send the data. It goes back to Earth.

Sometimes scientists tell me where to go. Sometimes I decide!

37°20'E
Yellowknife Bay
Darwin
Cooperstown
Kimberley
Aeolis Palus
Bagnold Dunes
Aeolis Mo
(Mount Sh
Pahrump Hills
Marias Pass
Bridger Basin
Naukluft Plateau
Gobabeb
Murray Buttes
MURRAY FORMATION
HEMATITE UNIT
CLAY UNIT
Sol 1750 Location
Ogunquit Beach
Vera Rubin Ridge
SULFATE UNIT

glossary & index

glossary

asteroids (AA-stuh-roydz) small, rocky objects that orbit the Sun

data (DAY-tuh) information used to learn about something

experiments (ik-SPAIR-uh-muhntz) carefully planned tests to discover something unknown or confirm understanding

navigate (NAA-vuh-gayt) to plan or control the path something takes

scientists (SYE-uhn-tists) people who study and do experiments to learn about the natural world

solar panels (SOH-luhr PAA-nuhlz) devices that change light into electricity

tread (TRED) the pattern of grooves on a tire

index